"I don't like poetry"

Robert Gillett
Beneath The Tracksuit

Poetry is boring

"Poetry is boring!"
No it's not.

"Poetry is crap!"
Not really though is it?

"Poetry is rubbish!"
Little narrow minded don't you think?

"Poetry is shit!"
How would you know?
You couldn't have read all of it.

"Emmmm"
Yeah, I thought so...

Robert Gillett

Poetry, of course may not be for everyone
but if you don't even give it a chance,
How will you ever know?

I don't like poetry

Contents

6. **Introduction**
7. **I don't like poetry**
10. I didn't like poetry
12. **Turning to poetry**
18. This time
20. **Using it for mental health**
24. Now it's not
25. Thought process
26. Hard enough
27. What's wrong
28. It's not that
30. Why can't I cry?
32. That dark night
34. I am depression
36. Chosen for you
37. **The discovery**
43. Hidden
44. More than a disability
46. **Breaking the stereotype**
48. Lad in a cap
49. Stereotypes of a poet
52. Are you sure you're not a rapper?
54. Beneath the tracksuit
57. **For mental health and more**
59. Art is art
60. Jumble
61. I lived in a tree
62. Was I lost?
63. The egg
64. Where are we actually
66. Who was the first?
68. Tim
70. Who makes the rules?

Robert Gillett

72. Share a moment
74. **Have a laugh with it**
76. Curry
77. Miracle cure
78. Karen
79. Kim
80. Sharon and Darren
82. You're so annoying
84. Tattoos and cigarette butts
86. Having a poo
88. If looks could kill
90. Remember remember
92. The teenage daughters boyfriend
94. Don't laugh
96. That doesn't go there
97. Today is today
98. **Writing for support**
99. You're still valid
100. Men know depression
102. There's no need for that
103. Mental health
104. My strength must survive
106. A conversation
108. Fall in line
109. **Writing for others**
111. I love you
112. Goodbye letter
114. I paint
116. You saved me
118. **A better outlook**
120. You don't like poetry
122. **For the record**
124. **A special thanks**

I don't like poetry

Introduction

First I'd like to thank you for purchasing this book and welcome you to my journey through poetry.

Whether you really like poetry or you don't, if you like it a little bit or don't give a shit about poetry, hopefully this book holds something for you.

There's a few mental health triggers in here, they may be a few tears. There's definitely a possibility of a smile and maybe even a laugh.

From a closet writer to an international seller.
From words on a page to an inspiration on the stage.

This is my story.

"I don't like poetry"

I don't like poetry

This may sound a little intense or cringy but for me, poetry became a game changer for my life and believe me if you knew me before my diagnosis, my mental health struggles, before I started writing then you probably wouldn't have ever thought I'd be saying those words.

Poetry became a place to laugh, cry, vent, giggle and be a little random. It brought me social circles, friends and support. Poetry helped with my confidence, my conversation skills and overcoming lots of anxiety. A lot of things started to change for me the day I picked up a pen.

Told you, "a little cringy".

It's a long way from "I don't like poetry".

Growing up I used to think poetry was pointless, irrelevant. It's not that it actually had a big effect on my life or caused me any problems in any way, I just thought it was shit. I related it to school and how boring I found it there. It was long days, draining lessons, teachers with coffee breath and short patience.

I didn't cope well in mainstream education. I always had a lot going on in my head and things going on around me in my life, so I had an unnecessary outlet. I was that cheeky chappy, one of the lads, annoying little twat at the back of the classroom making everyone laugh, with severe mental health issues that no one picked on.

Let's just say I didn't do too well at school.

Poetry was part of that, part of that school setting, along with science and all the other lessons I didn't pay attention to, especially English.

If any of my teachers read this, I am sorry for being a pain.

Learning Shakespeare and the sonnets he wrote, along with all the other historical poetry that they persisted in teaching us were rubbish, mostly written in ways no one can understand. It was a waste of time for me, that's how I felt back then anyway.

Maybe they should update it, make it more fun or relatable.

I suppose I then followed with that dim, narrow minded view of poetry growing into adulthood. I had that stereotypical opinion that poetry was boring. You mention poetry to people and you can literally see their face screw and their eyes roll a bit. It's funny. I was the same as this. I had the exact same look. I didn't really know why, most people wouldn't either. It's an automatic response to a lot of people. It's a response to the unknown or a view that counters theirs. That same view you get from many people when someone mentions vegan. It really can be funny to watch sometimes.

It's amazing how people's opinions change though.

Mine was a big change, I didn't like poetry, I thought it was actually quite stupid but here we are with my 3rd book.

It's definitely been a mindfulness journey with stereotypes broken, mindset changes and overcoming all different sorts of obstacles. It seems like a pretty random statement when you're talking about discovering poetry.

In all fairness it's a pretty random story but I'm glad you're here to read it.

I didn't like poetry

Growing up I didn't like poetry.
It's not that I hated it, it's not that I didn't respect it but I thought what we were taught was rubbish.
When I was 14, I should've been learning about poetry in my english class but I was too busy having a laugh or I was thinking about Britney's arse or her other naughty bits, not listening to this old dragon chatting about this poetry shit.
The words she's speaking were so boring.
It resembled my old man at home on the couch, he'd be snoring. I was a teenager, I'm more worried about my body transforming.
I didn't like poetry.

We're taught in school that poetry follows certain rules.
Growing up for me, school, poetry and rules really wasn't cool but did they teach us it all?
Was I just not listening?
Did I miss the part when someone poured out words from the heart or they laid out their beaten souls about a monster taking control or could I just not dissect the words like I can now,
I didn't like poetry.

Robert Gillett

Shakespeare and these other old folk wrote poetry in a language that I never spoke, I've got no qualms with this bloke but seriously these words were not for me.
Maybe because he died in 1616 or I didn't understand his sonnet that laid before me, 372 years after his death is the birth date of mine and his words were relevant in his time. I didn't understand his rhythm, I didn't understand his rhyme.
I didn't like poetry.

20 years later I am standing on stages, I'm filling up pages, I will listen, read, write this poetry shit for ages.
I love the rhythm, I love the rhyme, exploring the imagination from someone's unique mind.
What happened? Maybe nothing happened, maybe when I was 14 I should have paid attention in my English class, I shouldn't have been messing around or having a laugh and definitely not have been thinking about Britney's arse.
Because I actually like poetry.

I don't like poetry

Turning to poetry

When we're young, like really little, we're taught poetry in school. We never said we don't like poetry. We just learned the poems and got on with it, we'd enjoy it. We sit around on the carpet whilst the teacher reads poems to us and we learn them. I don't think I've ever heard a 5 year old say poetry is boring. Children are magical, they remember the words and proudly say them back to you. They take them home, excitedly share them with their parents. They read them in school events, happily.

Even now at 35 I can still remember a few from when I was really little.

Jack be nimble,
Jack be quick,
Jack jumped over the candlestick.

I have no idea what that poem is about but it's stuck with me for 30 years. It's funny how things do that, I remember the poem but I don't remember at 5 or 6 saying I didn't like poetry. I don't remember having a problem with it in primary school. I just learned the lines like everyone else.

Here's another one I remember.

Wee Willie Winkie runs through the town,
Upstairs and downstairs in his night-gown,
Tapping at the window, crying at the lock,
Are the children in their bed, for it's past ten o'clock?

I think I remember this one because of "Wee Willie Winkie". I must have been about 7 or 8 and Willie Winkie just made me laugh. That childish boy brain I had at that age has kept this poem with me. I have no idea what it's about or who even wrote it but I definitely remember it.

The next poem I remember I learnt I was about 13 years old. I can't remember where I learnt it but it's always stuck with me. It's a limerick, has an easy flow and is easy to remember. Lots of limericks I've come across and even quite a few I've written follow a similar style. I was a cheeky teenage boy so of course I was going to remember a poem like this one.

This one, it's a little bit, let's say it's a little bit naughty, rude or even worth a giggle. It depends how you take it.

No one said poetry didn't have a naughty side.

There was an old lady from Ealing

There was an old lady from Ealing,
She had a peculiar feeling,
She laid on her back,
Opened her crack,
She pissed all over the ceiling.

That's been locked in my head for 20+ years. I have no idea who wrote it so I can't give the credit but whoever did, definitely had a sense of humour.

A little story about that poem. I was at a church event decorating things for Christmas and a group there were writing limericks about Christmas. Somebody asked me if I knew any and I said "Yeah" and with a teenage boy cheeky grin (at 33), I said that poem out loud. People laughed and thought it was funny but after I read it, I realised where I was and I thought I probably shouldn't be reading that sort of poetry in church but it was taken well, so no harm done.

These things are pretty much all I remember about poetry from growing up and none of it is negative, so my opinion didn't need to change.

Robert Gillett

I think if they kept poetry in school relevant, engaging it would have a better impact on me. Maybe it was just me and my attitude towards the whole school setting but then why do so many people have a similar reaction to poetry like I did?

In our teenage years we had rap music and Eminem which was so much cooler than Shakespeare, maybe poetry just wasn't cool and everyone else had the same opinion as me, well the people who disregarded poetry anyway.

It's crazy how it changes, views change, you change, you pull back stereotypical views and actually open your eyes. Not just poetry but anything in life.

My change was my mental health. I fight depression, hard. Living with the disability I have makes this fight significantly harder. I take pills for this, have counselling for this and have developed a support group around this and of course I have my family but a major play in me opening up came from poetry. My hardest thought processes don't come out easily verbally but I found it became easier for me if I wrote them in verse.

My counsellor suggested I write a thought diary, which I did for a few weeks before I established that it was crap (For me). I was reading my daily diary of "I feel crap" "I'm so depressed" and it went like that, day after day. I couldn't find any positives from it. Who would? It was actually making me worse, looking back and reading how hard my week had been was doing more damage to me mentally.

One day I took a pen and a pad and sat on my bed and I just started putting words in verse, line after line, verse after verse, catch lines with rhymes. Hiding it from the Mrs. She saw me and looked at me confused and said,

"what are you doing?"

I nervously replied with scared eyes,

"I'm writing a poem"

I was stupidly embarrassed, why? Because I held the stigma that poetry was boring and for boring people and it wasn't a cool thing to do and it made me feel really silly, a little bit pathetic too

How stupid is that?

Robert Gillett

I was taking away what I was doing and quickly put a negative on it. That would have been completely counterproductive if I kept that thought. So I sat and I finished the poem.

I took my time and I pieced it all together slowly. I really put my all into it. I thought if I'm going to do it then I'm going to do it properly.

Eventually I finished and it was such a surreal feeling. I'm 30 years old and I wrote a poem, I put my emotions on paper and it was a mental release.

I had taken a thought process of what I was thinking and I made something from it. It was something I could be proud of and I am so glad I went through that moment and all of those emotions because it's helped me get to where I am today. It all happened for a reason and it started right there.

This poem actually got picked up quickly on social media and was featured in the "MS Focus" Magazine in the US. I was so proud, I wrote something in a mental struggle in my corner of Cornwall and a few weeks later it had been published in a magazine across the world.

This Time

There was no accident,
Not this time,
Friends and Family say "you're gonna be fine",
How do they know?
They're not me!
Is it in my head or just insanity?

There's no denying it,
Not this time,
Not even the doctors can say it's fine.
I froze,
Dead still,
Couldn't even blink.
Am I dying?
A stroke?
What would you think?

A new day,
More tests,
What this time?
Needles and scans,
Fluids from the spine!
I'm nervous,

I'm angry,
I'm scared to say the least.
What am I fighting?
What is this beast?

Test after test,
I got my results this time.
The problem is me,
I'm broken,
Stupid brain of mine.
It's scarred,
Signals blocked,
It's Multiple Sclerosis.
What now?
How am I going to fight this?

Don't give up,
I need to be strong this time!
Quitting is not an option,
Not when there is a mountain to climb
I'm frightened and it breaks me
But MS I can beat,
I am a warrior within that nothing can defeat.

Using it for mental health

Depression is a hard fight, it has been quite persistent in my life, anxiety too but I didn't really understand that I was struggling until my mid 20s. I figured it was more the way life was. I didn't know any difference so I thought it quite normal to feel the way I was. It wasn't until I actually started speaking to professionals when I found out my thought processes needed looking at.

I've been to counselling numerous times, had numerous different people talk to me about mental health and try to help pull me out of these depressive states I find myself in.

I've had quite a few one to one sessions with different counsellors, I've been on two different CBT (cognitive behavioural therapy) courses. I've taken other courses too to help with my mental health. I take antidepressants, tried and tested my way through them to figure out which ones work right for me (I'm currently taking sertraline). I have amazing emotional support at home but I still found myself crashing.

I think talking was my biggest issue for not helping myself. I didn't like speaking out, I didn't like being open and honest about how I was feeling. I felt it made me look weak. I still struggle with it now but I'm so much better than I was before.

After I wrote "This time" it became a habit. Taking my mental struggles and putting them in a verse. I was making full works out of painful thoughts and emotions. It became a new way to communicate my feelings, eventually.

Being brought up in a world where men don't talk about their feelings was an issue and I held that. So I didn't share my poetry with anyone but I could write it and read it and be proud of what I'd made. It became the best place to vent or make sense of the mess in my head.

Even now if I'm struggling I take myself off and I string words and verses together and I make art from it.

I can explain on paper so much more than what comes out of my mouth. There's something about the quiet screams in my head that make more sense on paper than they do verbally, so I continue to use poetry as my go to when I'm struggling.

Some of what I write, especially when I first started writing, is full of pain. My poems can be filled with a lot of self hatred, a lot of painful rhetorical questions and can be very hard to read back but I'm so pleased with every one of them that I've finished. It's a weird sense of achievement that I can actually read back what I was going through. I kept writing once I started and I kept reading them back and it was working.

It still helps now.

I highly recommend it.

I began sharing it online and believe me that took a lot of persuasion. The Mrs was telling me it could help others, make them feel less alone. I wasn't 100 on this but I agreed.

I run under the pseudonym "Beneath The Tracksuit" because that's where the struggle is, that's where the pain is. I have this disability that you can't see and it all hides beneath the tracksuit because I'm always wearing a tracksuit. They're so comfortable and easy to get on and off so the name came naturally. One of my first poems was called "Beneath the tracksuit" and the name sort of became apparent from then.

Sharing opened a whole world of vulnerability but I stuck it out and followers grew soon after. I had thousands of people reaching out to me, I still do. They're all telling they feel the same or thanking me for putting their pain into words. It made me feel so much less alone in the fight I go through.

I appreciate these people that are there, that follow me, that watch my journey, it's become a massive lift for me mentally in this life with depression, in this life living with multiple sclerosis.

I would have never imagined that my painful words could have me connected to people all around the world but it did. I would have never have thought that my struggle in verse would help others but it did.

I could share whole books with you with poetry I have written in a bad mental state or on a rough day but this book is about the journey so I'll share a couple of my expressive verses and we'll continue the journey.

Some of the next few poems may be a bit hard to read or may be a trigger but it's where I take my pain, like I said before, It's like getting the mess out of the head.

I don't like poetry

Now it's not

It's there then it's not,
A smile beaming,
A happy laugh,
Joyous moment,
Was there, now it's not.

Robert Gillett

A thought process

A daily battle of thoughts and fights,
Twisted self indulgence of an attacking mind,
Take a smile away and replace it with dread,
Can't hide from the thoughts attacking the head.
Depressive and repetitive deep in the cerebrum,
Loud and aggressive,
A harrowing drum.
Anxiously waiting for horrid contemplation,
Emotions leaving the body,
Mentality is breaking.

Hard enough

The disability is hard enough without the abundance of judgement caused by an irrelevant flexing their arrogance.

The depression is hard enough without the sligh sighs and rolling eyes from devil's in disguise.

The struggle is hard enough without the pain gained each day trying to portray life in a typical way.

Life is hard enough without the disability mentally draining me and challenging me physically.

What's wrong?

It's ups and downs,
It's the somethings wrong,
It's that feeling I no longer belong,

It's mental health,
Depression and internal sorrow,
Strong today but broken tomorrow.

It's the disability,
It worked yesterday but not today,
It's the independence being slowly snatched away.

It's the judgement,
People stare and they accuse,
Like this is an image that someone would choose.

It's the hurt,
Families quietly watching someone fade.
Loved ones standing by absorbing the pain.

It's the man in the mirror,
The one crying at night,
Wondering the ways of how he can fix his life.

It's not that

It's not that I'm not listening,
My brain struggles to consume.

It's not that I don't know how,
My body sometimes can't compute.

Sometimes I haven't got the strength,
It's not that I just won't do.

Occasionally I physically can't,
It's not that I choose not to.

It's not that I'm lazy,
I live with constant fatigue.

It's not that I'm pathetic or weak,
I have these pains that run through me.

I have trouble with my thinking,
It's not that I'm messed up.

I struggle with mental health,
It's not that I gave up.

Robert Gillett

Somethings I must do different,
It's not that I actually changed.

I always do the best I can,
It's not that I planned to be this way.

Why can't I cry?

Why can't I cry?
I'm lost,
It's bad luck,
Loss in body trust,
It keeps giving up,
My mental health can't keep up.
I'm digging out of hell but I can't reach to the top,
The end light keeps drifting or am I still sinking,
I have no hope left,
My sanity goes right but i'm passing left,
Suicide or breakfast what a fucking thought process,
I'm not sure how much fight I have left.
I'm lost.
When I feel myself falling away I need catching but I'm too proud to shout so I fall in silence,
Though the tough days and the tense days I keep it hidden and it stays,
I stay in pain,
Too many emotions locked away in my brain.
Why ain't I shouting,
Why can't I cry?
I'm left lost contemplating different ways to die.
Why can't I cry?

Robert Gillett

I need help but I can't ask,
I'm not allowed to ask,
I'm a man bury this shit deep,
My emotions shouldn't be weak so I continue to mask.
I'm my own worst enemy but I'm the only one inside my head that knows what's going on with me,
I'm crashing in there,
I feel I'm going crazy but I shut the door behind as I walked into the self sabotage and no one can understand me.
I look so calm and I'm face filled with smiles,
So no one knows,
No one understands,
Why can't I let them know?
Why can't I cry?

I don't like poetry

That dark night

That dark night falls in,
Windows are closed with the drapes drawn,
Doors bolted,
Heating alight to protect against bitter ice setting in.
Familiar faces,
Their loving embraces,
Not a more treasured place,
A crowd in the abode,
So why do you feel alone?

House is filled with light and personality,
It's still dark out of your eyes,
A dimmer switch only for you.
Voices are in a peaceful motion,
Yet you feel commotion,
Isolated condemnation,
Emotions are broken.

Tearful yet tearless,
Tears should be running down the face like the rain crashing against the window pain,
Instead the face runs dry,
Nor a resemblance of a broken cry,

Robert Gillett

Passing thoughts for that disappearing twinkle that used to fill the eye.

Your soft temperament and nice nature is replaced with the anger of an ogre,
Invisible to see,
Fraudulent joy sits on your posture,
A half witted smile the face holds,
A forever unruly fronting of an internal mans worn,
The depression's surface is peaceful but the inside is distorted and torn.

The dark night falls in,
Windows are closed with the drapes drawn.

I don't like poetry

I am Depression

I'm a Devil that gets trapped in someone's body,
You would be shook if you come across me,
I snatch pieces from an innocent identity,
I'm greedy,
I'll take everything from within thee,
I need you to feed me,
Your mental distortion will make this easy.
I'm planning to break you,
Take from within you,
I'll whisk that smile away and consume the best of you!
You're not escaping,
I'll get claws buried in you so deep you won't sleep,
Leave you with horrifying thoughts these nightmares will keep you out of deep.
I'll take your friends from you,
Your job from you,
Your wife from you,
I'll take your whole fucking life from you.
Your humanoid man made pills will be no rescue.
Your CBT therapy tries to suppress me but reality I'm here for eternity.
You can try "chin up, good boy, tomorrow will be better"
But I'm still here,

Robert Gillett

Still here dripping poison in the ear,
Loser,
Fat,
Ugly,
Look at the state of your face,
You're a waste of fucking space,
You can try to fight me, suppress me, neglect me,
You can't escape me.
You can try to survive this strife eating you from the inside,
My mission is to destroy you without a single care,
I am Depression,
I'm not going anywhere.

Chosen for you

The carnage and terror that holds centre of the depressive mind are dimensions apart from the serenity and tranquillity that many seem to find.
An appearance holds an unknown truth from the reality of the catastrophe that someone is fighting inside.
It's an unbalanced,
Unhinged,
Unkind type of mind.
There's no escape.
No escaping into the emptiness,
No running from the beast that has its claws in you.
This is man's eternal battle and it was built to last but man was built to endure these unforgivable tasks leaving a physiological mask,
Leaving an image chosen by a broken man.
An unsuspecting opposing vision of war or inner man's fight.
You see light,
Not the depressive grip squeezing the life out of someone from the inside.
The image you see is chosen for you.

Robert Gillett

The Discovery

What happened next to me was such an eye opener, I couldn't really believe it. I still had the thought that I didn't really like poetry. I didn't like it because I still related it to school and exams and it was boring, blah, blah, blah.

Even though I was using poetry to help me with my mental health and I had connected with people across the world with words in verse I still had a narrow view of poetry. I said daft things like "I write poetry but I don't really like poetry".

I was offered the opportunity to perform my poetry on stage to a crowd at a poetry-spoken word event. Of course I said no at first. Hiding behind a pseudonym and having people read your words online is a million miles away from putting your emotions on stage to a crowd. I was terrible at talking and always felt really vulnerable when I did actually get around to talking, so why on earth would I get on stage and read my words, my pain, my expressive verses to a crowd of people? I don't know?

With a bit of persuasion,

"You can raise awareness"

"You can help others"

Again I agreed. I thought, if it can help one person then it'll be worth it.

I read at my local open stage first, "open stage Bodmin" a warm up to the poetry event. It was full of musicians, singers and a variety of other acts, it was all such a blur, anxiety definitely took over.

Mimi, The compère there was very inviting and supportive, she tried to ease me but that wasn't happening. I sat in a world of anxiety all night until I read my first poem on stage. I hid behind my phone, stuttering my words and it was over so fast. I had waves of applause but I completely dismissed it. I couldn't believe I did it though I was proud for a moment but mental health really wouldn't let me take it in. The reality of it, I actually felt a little stupid, embarrassed. I tried to hang on to the positive in it but it was so hard.

It's crazy when I think back to my first performance and how terrified I was and how poorly I read but we all start new journeys somewhere and who knew it would be the beginning of something.

Robert Gillett

A few days later, the spoken word event was at the same venue, organised by an established spoken word company "SproutSpoken". This one made me more anxious than before because I was sharing the stage with actual poets and people that write a lot and perform it on the regular.

I went to the event, not really knowing what to expect. I didn't like poetry, even though I was writing it so to be honest I thought it was going to be boring. I thought I'd listen to a few people, then read my 2 poems then leave.

I was completely wrong.

The whole event changed my view on poetry.

A poet went on stage, read a few and came off. Then the next and the next. Each and every time someone took the stage I became more engrossed. Nobody was talking in a language I didn't know, everyone was reading about life and stories about what they'd been through or about absolute randomness.

It was so engaging and kept me really drawn to the whole experience, which I definitely didn't expect

Then I went up, sat on a chair because I don't really do standing much (Thanks MS) especially when I'm in troubled states and I was anxious as fuck.....

I hid behind my phone, just like last time, I don't think I looked up once. I anxiously read two poems, two painful poems which I had written in a struggle and I was given a tremendous applause, I couldn't believe it. It was such a surreal feeling. My pain and heartbreaking words had received a reaction in real time, it had me beaming with smiles. It was a next level feeling.

The anxiety and the adrenaline cooled off nicely and I felt incredible. I didn't know this could have such an impact on me.

A poet that came on a few after me really helped me change my whole opinion of what poetry was and how I should look at it.

Paul Temme, this guy is an incredible poet. He took to the stage and his whole aura had me hooked. He read a poem called "Music for the masses" but he didn't just read a poem, he fucking smashed it! He proudly held himself on stage, book in one hand and he had the audience in the other. Eye contact with everyone in front of him, no slipping of words and he read verse after verse, without a stutter or anything misspoken. He had brilliant expressions and the whole poem was captivating. It was nothing short of amazing.

He finished to a roar of applause and I was mesmerised at how he just did that. I said,

"I wanna be like him"

I was 32 years old and felt like a teenage fan boy wanting to be David Beckham. His performance was epic and was quickly something I aspired to be like as a performer.

I thought if I'm going to do this, I've got to do it properly. I needed to drop those stereotypical views I had because it's all stupid. I wanted to put myself to work and put myself out there, like he just did.

I had a message, I've got words of support and pain and struggle and people need to hear them. I thought if I could do what he just did then I might actually be able to reach people that need support and tell them it's ok, it's ok to be sad, it's ok to be depressed, it's ok to be disabled. Most of all, it's something that I could do for myself, something really positive out of my pain. Maybe this whole "Poetry" thing could actually be really good for me. I started from there, I wanted to take my words and I want to own the stage like Paul Temme did.

I wanted to do more with this, I knew I could do more than this.

I'd been using my poetry as an escape for my mental health, I'd been living in a world of disability and depression. I still do but I'm so much more than that and I think poetry helped me show myself despite what has been happening to me and what I was going through, I could be more than that.

I could use the pain and create something more.

Hidden

There's hidden depths in you somewhere that you didn't know you had,
It could take one different path to discover what's hidden in you.

More than a disability

I live with a disability,
I am a disabled man,
This disability isn't all that I am.
I stand a bit crooked,
I struggle to walk,
Sometimes I slur when I talk.
I have a walking stick,
I don't move very far,
I do my shopping in those annoying mart karts.
I am a disabled man.

I'm a father,
I raise my children to the best of my ability,
Doing everything I can to still make it silly.
I changed the nappies,
Taught them to speak,
Took them to school for their first week.
I'm there when they need me,
For a laugh or for a cry,
I'll always be there for them until the day that I die.
I may be disabled but I'm still a father.

Robert Gillett

I'm a partner,
I swept this woman off her feet,
I kept getting her drunk until she fell in love with me.
We're a team her and me,
We share dreams and troubles,
Life's stupid carfuffle,
I confide in her and she confides when I'm not asleep.
I think I make her happy,
I must because she puts up with my grief.
I may be disabled but I'm still a partner.

I can be a bit daft,
I'm a bit of a man child,
I'll do little things to achieve a cheeky smile.
I'm a dog owner,
I've got my own little Teddy bear,
If I'm having a bad day my little fluff ball is always there.
I'm a good friend,
A doting father,
A loving partner.
I may be a disabled man but this disability isn't all that I am.

Breaking the stereotype

Some people have a narrow minded view on how poets are, what they look like, how they behave and the things they do. I was personally guilty of that one. I used to think poetry was boring and for boring people.

It's so random how society can stereotype someone. There's literally pages and pages of stereotypes of a poet online and they don't really make sense to me. I read through them and I found that some poets I know may relate to a few of those things but so does everyone else in society. Some of the things were so random and some stupid, others just really funny. It was definitely a weird read but it made a good poem.

Another stereotype, Men are weak if they talk about their emotions.

This is utter shit!

Anybody who is struggling should be allowed to reach out, regardless of your age or gender. Problems shared are a big release and become easier to be solved if you speak out. If you're bottling up broken emotions and struggling in silence it doesn't lead down a helpful path. It takes a brave person to reach out for support, it takes a strong person to ask for help. Just because someone talks about things or behaves in a way that's not typical of the way things seem to be in mainstream society doesn't necessarily need to be a bad thing.

After I started writing, sharing and performing I dropped stereotypes, broke stereotypes and showed others it's ok to not be ok and it's ok to speak out. I think this may be one of the reasons why people are drawn to me.

I'm a young man and I'm open. I talk about my emotions and my difficulties. I wear tracksuits and I don't particularly fit into stereotypical brackets that much of society seems to hold for someone like me. I'm a disabled performance poet that battles with mental health issues daily and I get on stage to share my pain with the world as a release and it does me wonders. I'm not what mainstream society sees as a disabled man, a depressed man, or even as a poet. The amount of times people have told me that I should be a rapper is unreal. I just be myself, real, I wouldn't do this any other way.

There's nothing wrong with being different as long as you're always being yourself.

Lad in a cap

There was once a lad in a cap,
He used to say poetry was crap,
He then discovered words could explain pain in a verse,
And that was the end of that.

Robert Gillett

Stereotypes of a poet

Not all poets are die hard protesters,
We don't all stand there with boards on picket lines,
It's not a necessity to tell people how to be politically correct in life.
Some stay out of it and think protests are shit,
Others protest from home,
Fill out campaign forms on their phones,
Some simply want their views to be left alone,
But some poets are die hard protesters.

Not all poets are boring,
Some might not be for you and write about leaves and trees or bees and their honey,
Whilst others are simply just fucking funny,
Some poets set their farts on fire,
Some party to states of dire,
I know a few poets who do it for the crack,
Some poets smoke crack,
Some keep you engaged,
Maybes make you weep,
Not all poets put you to sleep.
But some poets are boring.

Not all poets stink,
Most of us shower most days,
Or wear some sensual aftershave,
We don't all have garlic breath,
With armpits that are not too fresh,
No aroma that resembles a fish,
Not all poets smell like shit,
But some poets do stink.

Not all poets went to uni or have an A level education,
It's not a rule to need a college degree to have a passion for poetry,
Some of us dropped out of school at 15,
Fell into poetry in our 30s,
Couldn't figure it out in school but now use words as a tool or as a way to express the mess in the head.
Some poets don't like education, think it's a pointless task,
Only attended school because it's a society ask.
But some poets went to uni and have an A level education.

Not all poets are vegan,
Some of us eat burgers,
Others only eat fish,
Some munch out on a tofu dish,
Some are vegetarian,

Robert Gillett

Others pescatarian,
I'm a don't care what I eat aterian,
But some poets are vegan.

Not all poets live in an ivory tower,
We're not all rich and live in castles,
Have moats in our front yard,
Have a butler called bill,
Be a distance relative to prince will,
Some of us live in flats,
Maybe a 3 bedroomed house,
Or a tiny studio with just enough room for a mouse,
They might live in a terraced house not far from your street,
Or even in that council estate where you wouldn't plant your feet.
But some poets might live in an ivory tower.

So many stereotypes of a poet just made up by people who think they know it but you never know,
Oneday at a protest rally about the stereotypes of a poet, you might come across a stupidly boring, grotesquely smelling, highly intelligent vegan poet who lives in an ivory tower.

Are you sure you're not a rapper?

No, I'm not a rapper,
Yeah, I wear a tracksuit and snapback,
I've got lush trainers with my name on the back,
I stroll with a stick but to go with it?
I've got swagger
But that doesn't make me a rapper.

No, I'm not a rapper.
Yeah, I wear a chain,
Silver belch that hangs around my neck,
Got a matching one for the wrist,
Usually looking swarve because I've been to the barbers and got a sweet trim,
You might say I even look a little dapper,
But that doesn't make me a rapper.

No, I'm not a rapper.
Yeah, My language can be a little controversial,
My music volume may be a little bit annoying for you,
I do write lyrics and take them to a stage,
I may even curse in a verse,
Or chat bars to a crowd that ain't the traditional manner,
But it doesn't make me a rapper.

Robert Gillett

No, I'm not a rapper,
Yeah, Robbie rhymes with Plan B, Master P, Jamie T, Jay Z,
Eazy-e, Snoop d o double g,
Like them I've got a back story that some would struggle to believe.
I've got a world of pain burning inside me.
I turned to words and became a lyrical hacker.
But that still doesn't make me a rapper.

No, I'm not a rapper.
You're putting me in a box with that stereotypical lock,
A tracksuit, a snapback, treds and a chain,
Owning lyrics and taking the stage,
A cheeky personality and an awesome name,
And rolling round with bags of swagger,
These things don't even make a rapper a rapper.

I don't like poetry

Beneath The Tracksuit

Beneath The Tracksuit I was broken.
I'm not ashamed to share I felt damaged beyond repair,
Which left me in despair,
It broke me,
It crushed me from the inside,
Damaged the pathways for the brain waves to help me think straight,
To help me operate,
I needed to find a way to survive each day and live my life my way,
This new point of reality for me.
I crumbled beyond belief,
I watched my support leave,
My friends leave,
But I gritted my teeth and I refused to lose whilst walking on this path,
This path I didn't choose,
I hid my pain behind a smile,
Kept my head up and my tears behind the eyes,
It's my life that I despised,
My mental health,
My disability,
I just wanted to be free.

Robert Gillett

Beneath The Tracksuit I felt a world of judgement,
People with death stare eyes that choose despise are now disrupting my life,
They're Adding to the strife.
30 years old I became a depressed disabled man,
But I choose to succeed,
I'm doing the best I can and people don't like it,
Like mental thoughts I just have to fight this,
I can't tear myself apart piece after piece feeding this depressive beast,
I'm done with fighting,
Fighting the anxiety,
Fighting the Depression,
Fighting peoples judgement,
I have pain in abundance,
I didn't deserve this injustice,
I didn't cause this,
There's no need for the moralistic man with the slurs in the streets or the twisted individual thats lives with me and slurs me from beneath,
Just leave me be.
There's a whole world beneath the surface,
There's a whole reality they will never see,
Stay away with your misconceptions,
Please just leave me to be me.

I don't like poetry

Beneath The Tracksuit I was a lost soul but I found words,
I found my way to a page to express the pain that's invading my brains,
I became open with my emotions and the poetry was set in motion,
Words became my ocean,
My sea of release,
Just me and a breeze,
Sailing free,
I became free,
The years of self torture and curse where looking back at me
But in a verse,
I saw a world of pain,
I was putting years of tears into pages,
Sentences filled with savage words and internal rages,
I had made this,
I made beauty from hurt,
Turned destruction into rhyme,
This is my time,
My time to be me.

Robert Gillett

From mental health to more

Growth was always going to happen with poetry, especially once I dropped the stereotypes. I wanted it to happen, I was making it happen. I absolutely loved writing and performing and seeing others perform so growth came naturally.

I started writing about more, having fun with words and using it for other things. It became a great way of dealing with those messed up, weird thoughts and those strange 3 am thoughts that keep your brain awake or even making sense of those random conversations that end up with no real answer.

Poetry became fun and not only a tool to express the painful mess that over clouds me.

Words began pouring out of my head daily. Verses, rhymes, poems, lyrics, all about the most random things and I just rolled with it. I wasn't going to argue with myself about what art was.

Personally I love the 3am poetry that comes out. It's always the most random things about aliens, the universe, things that are so random and there's no one to talk to about it because everyones asleep so I just jot words that sometimes end up as poetry. Sometimes it's absolute nonsense but we can't always win everytime.

Questions and conversations that don't really have answers that are just proper random, you know the conversations that don't happen everyday but are really fun to have, that don't make sense or have an obvious answer. They make good poems too.

Poetry helped me connect with the randomness of life.

The whole artform started to become an adventure if you like. I was exploring and experimenting but going with the flow and taking every day as it came and I was really enjoying what I'd discovered.

I turned poetry into a hobby, that's a million miles away from "I don't like poetry"

Robert Gillett

Art is art

Art is art.
No matter the style,
No matter the format,
It's still art,
It's your art.
Nobody can discredit yours because it's yours,
Your art not anybody else's.
So you can't be wrong,
It will never be pointless,
It's not a waste.
It's amazing.
It's your expression,
Your unique vision,
Your creation,
Your imagination,
It's your art.

Jumble

Ocsolcanilay petory smpliy is a jmbule of wrods taht olny wudfonerl popele wlil udnertsnad.

Robert Gillett

I lived in a tree

I once wished I lived in a tree,
So high just me and the leaves,
What if I fell out?
Hit the floor with a clout?
Who would be there to find me?

Was I lost

Was I lost? It's all blank.
Did I lose my ability?
Did someone steal my memory?

Was I lost? It's all gone.
Was I dead in my sleep?
Had I fallen too deep?

Was I lost? It's missing.
It's only a black world of nothingness,
Today is the same as the rest.

Was I lost? I can't find it.
I can't be alone in this,
There must be others with dreams they miss.

Robert Gillett

The egg

Was it the chicken or was it the egg?
The annoying question that infiltrates the head.
Chickens lay eggs and out comes the chicken,
Why the confusion?
The origin isn't really missing!
Chickens are a product of evolution and growth but
dinosaurs laid eggs 65 million years ago.
The egg came first and the foetus evolved into a chick,
That answer is simple but society's brain struggles to answer it.
It was the chicken that came out of the egg and the egg came first,
Good luck trying to figure out what laid it, was it a dinosaur or was it some other random bird.

Now go to sleep...

I don't like poetry

Where are we actually?

Did a big bang actually come from nothing?
A bang of nothingness that caused rocks to clash,
Cemented together now binded forever.

Was our world actually created by a tremendous accident?
Are we actually gliding through space 500 thousand miles an hour?
Why isn't it making my hair go nuts?
Why ain't it making my eyes water?

Are we actually locked in the atmosphere of this rocky ball and I spend half my life upside down and I don't even fall?
Did I miss something?

Are we actually spinning a thousand miles an hour and not getting dizzy?
I don't feel like I'm moving and I'm not feeling sick.
I don't understand it!

Did life actually begin on earth from deserted plains and isolated seas sprouting into an abundance of life and towering trees?

Robert Gillett

Are we actually an evolution from monkeys?
Then why are they still here and why can't they understand me?
Why can't I swing from tree to tree?

Are we actually descendents from the mesopotamian people?
Did they actually evolve and walk 5000 miles, swim across the oceans so I could be before you?

What actually happened?
I ain't got a clue and this sounds a little too good to be the truth.....

Who was the first?

Have you ever wondered who was first and just, Why???
Who was the first that did it and why on earth would you do that?

The first person to milk a cow and drink it,
Did they see this beast in the fields feeding its young?
At that moment did they decide that they had to have some?
Did they look a cow's udders dripping and give it a little squeeze,
Love the taste so much,
They made different variants like yoghurt and cheese.
How on earth did they explain it to their mates?
"see that cow in the field, I've been drinking its juices and it's great"
"let's take the milk from this cow's boobs and put it in all our food"
That first guy would have looked crazy.

The first fertiliser,
Someone saw a horse do a poo and thought it was a good idea to rub it all over his food,
Bask their seeds in an animals mess,
Leave it there and hope for the best.

Robert Gillett

They would have had to do that on the sly,
Could you imagine if they told someone there was horse shit in their pie.
How would they explain that?
"Look at my potatoes, they're huge, they've been out there for weeks covered in your horse's poop".
That guy was crazy as well.

The first bungee jumper,
He must have been drunk or mad,
Maybe a death wish he had,
Or a great idea to conquer a fear.
"Let's tie our feet to a rope and jump off the bridge and hope. You could be stranded in mid air or fall to your death but this is a theory that we really need to test".
Why do you test that?
Why would you wanna go first?

Some people do things that seem a proper crazy but somehow it works,
Like the guy that invented skydiving,
It looks awesome but you wouldn't have caught me going first.

I don't like poetry

Tim

There was a young boy called finn,
No older than twelve,
He was strangely quite short,
About the size of an elf.

Finn liked to sit out at night and stare amongst the stars,
Spending hours wondering how alone we are.
Then one night, alone on his porch,
A figure appeared covering the light of his touch.

A little green man,
Little but still taller than Finn,
Had big bead like eyes and was terribly thin.
He spoke in a familiar way and to Finn he did say,
*"I'm from Saturn's moon Titan,
I'm an Intergalactic Martian".*

"Titans Intergalactic Martian" excitingly replied Finn,
"I know what, We can call you Tim"
It seemed like Tim and Finn could be the best of friends,
Finn wanted to explore the universe on adventures that didn't seem to end.

Robert Gillett

Sadly for Finn he never got to go on any adventures or tell anyone about Tim and the wonder he's just seen,
It turns out Tim was actually quite mean.

Tim had came down to earth to get himself some food,
The thing that tastes best are children in a good mood,
"You should never happily approach strangers" Tim said,
As he opened his mouth and bit off Finn's head.

Who makes the rules?

You drive through fields, glorious, endless grassy fields, vibrantly spring green. There's lambs and cows, Strolling around freely as they go, munching on the grass, not a care in the world. No worries.

You're delivering canned dog food to the RSPCA. Damaged animals are now safe. Your dog food contains beef and lamb. All soaked in gravy, perfect for a rescued dog,

How is that right? You drive past one to feed it to another. That leaves questions. Thought processes that you can't process that end up with more questions and more to process, What the fuck? Who makes the rules on this? You can keep a dog as a pet and feed it lamb or beef or chicken or prawn. If you keep a cow as a pet you wouldn't feed it a cat or rat, or dog. You'd feed it the grass from the green lawns.

Who makes the rules? You'd let a cat eat a mouse but won't let a mouse in our house. You'd rescue and feed a stray cat, why not that wondering rat? You will save a dirty dog, pet, love and feed that broken dog but not a stinky hogg.

Robert Gillett

Why? Who makes the rules? You save some, breed some, free some, release some, yet feed some to the others. They don't have a choice and they don't make the rules. It leaves more questions, more to process, Who actually makes the rules? Animals get what they can take or take what they're given. As a human society how are our rules written?

The Chinese eat bats and rats and dogs and cats. The French eat frog legs and fat snails and in Iceland they eat killer whales. Egyptians eat elephant fish from the river Nile. In Singapore, I don't know how they do it but they eat crocodiles. Australian tribes eat camels and kangaroos, in the Republic of Congo they eat chimpanzees, they eat monkeys too, In Japan they eat bears, they eat dolphins as well. All these animals I wouldn't eat myself.

I couldn't eat a dolphin burger, couldn't imagine a crocodile sandwich, A kangaroo curry. I couldn't bbq a rat, have bear on my full english or stir fry monkey or have camels on toast, I wouldn't have whales with my roast. I won't make bolognese with a bat or have a sweet n sour cat. I couldn't kebab a chimpanzee tail or make soup from a snail.
I know some of this might sound a little cruel but don't blame me,
I didn't make the rules.

Share a moment

You share your life with strangers,
An abundance of people walking their own paths.
They're living their way and unknowingly will share
moments in time with you.
If you simply sat and paused to just watch,
Just see the people in front of you,
The mum pushing her pushchair,
The cyclist in lycia in a rush to get nowhere.
The businessman sad faced carrying their briefcase,
The smiling homeless man in the abandoned shop doorway.
The observing tourist from a distant land,
The ageing couple hobbling hand in hand.
All strangers unnamed to you.

Have you ever wondered how they got there?
Or where they're going?
They all have a story behind them,
Mistakes and heartbreaks,
Romance and keepsakes,
Success and headaches,
Achievements and life breaks,
A life unknown to you.

Robert Gillett

They have planned futures and different pasts,
All on a different path leading up to this moment,
A moment of time you will all share.
No one knows that you're there and they don't know of each other.
Take one breath and this moment of time is gone forever.

Joining your past memories and life's previous entries,
This moment disappears,
This moment in time is gone forever.
It's a collective reminder that no moment lasts forever and you all shared it as strangers.

Have a laugh with it

Poetry can be so funny. Once I found the funny side to it, I couldn't wait to get stuck in. The humour that hides in the poetry world is so underrated. I've seen poets on stage that have had me in absolute stitches, I've read so many funny poems too. Limericks normally have a laugh out loud moment.

Poetry can hold plenty of jokes and can be set all around humour, so much of it is waiting to be discovered.

The way poetry and comedy can come together is so clever. It's not heard of enough. If many people could actually see the funny side of poetry a bit more, I can assure you more people would probably think twice about sidelining a poetry night.

They become fun to write, having people laughing at something you've written is brilliant. When they're laughing with you and not at you definitely helps too.

When I started "trying" to write funny poems, I used real life situations or little jokes in limericks and the random things in life that made me laugh. It was a whole different place to write.

I'm up for a laugh, I have this whole cheeky chappy way of life. Not many people see it too much because I normally write in a struggle. I'm sure if people only knew me through my poetry and the places I've reached out to, they would probably think I'm constantly depressed but that's far from the truth. Poetry was normally the go to thing to do in a struggle but I'm so much more than that.

I spent so much time putting all of my pain into verse, it was a big adjustment trying to be funny with it but I'm genuinely a funny guy and normally up for a laugh so I thought to just have fun with it, what was the worst thing that could happen?

It's not as if I got on stage and the whole room went completely silent and awkward when they didn't understand the joke.....

I'm gonna share some with you here but I must warn you, some are a little rude, some are a little daft, some just silly and some you might find not so funny but it's all good fun.

Curry

Someone took me out for a curry,
I ate that beast in a hurry,
I shouldn't eat vindaloo,
Later on I followed through,
Next time I'll go for a mcflurry.

Robert Gillett

Miracle cure

Dr Sningulflerp knocked at my door,
And promised me a miracle cure,
I called him a disgrace,
Punched him in the face,
Hopefully he won't knock anymore.

Karen

Moaning is this woman's talent,
Her opinions are always apparent,
She's difficult to please,
Always giving everyone grief,
We all know a lady called Karen.

"Sorry to all the Karens out there"

Robert Gillett

Kim

There was a lady called Kim,
She put hair removal cream on her minge,
She got Dave to give it a blow as it was starting to glow,
Now she's been left all singed.

Sharon n Darren

I know this woman called Sharon,
She married a guy called Darren,
He shew another woman his dick,
So Sharon stabbed it with a stick,
Now Darren's penis is baron.

Sorry for the rude limericks...

Got to experiment though, right?

You're so annoying

You build inside,
In silence,
Different to the similar that you know that are coming,
You come out loud,
Instantly proud,
Echoing the air that surrounds.
People don't know whether to cringe out or walk away,
Some people stare and others just laugh,
You're so annoying,
You noisy unexpected fart.

Hidden swirls of dusts,
Blended together like a planets,
Crossing vasts amounts of space,
You always take form somewhere,
Refusing to be a waste,
Do you land there or simply grow?
Truth is I don't really know,
You always appear for no reason apparent to me,
You're so annoying,
You hanging flappy bogey.

Robert Gillett

Normally you hide,
Hide like a dim light at the end of a tunnel,
Different shades of orange and yellow,
Like a spring meadow,
Maybe the last hope for a candle,
Occasionally you squeeze out to be seen,
You squeeze to reach the forefront,
Reaching through the cracks,
You're so annoying,
You flaky escaping earwax.

You're a muted climber,
Silently creeping like a spider,
Overcoming obstacles through terrain not built for you,
Where did you spawn from?
Your colour normally leaves a clue but it seems impossible,
At the least improbable.
You seem invincible,
You're made of magical tuff stuff,
You're so annoying,
Fucking belly button fluff.

I don't like poetry

Tattoos and cigarette butts

Cornwall is such a beautiful place to be,
Glorious golden beaches and endless waves of sea.

One thing here needs to be made aware,
These fucking seagulls,
Nobody warned you they're there.

They're bigger than the average I'm sure,
I've never seen bad boys like these before.
They're strolling down the boardwalk,
Not bothered by the passers-by,
These fuckers walk the street in gangs,
They're not governed like other birds that stay flying high.

These look like they're on steroids,
They're proper buff,
They're too hard for smoking,
They just chew the cigarette butts.

I swear I saw on once,
He had fucking tattoos,
He was sizing me up,
Looking to eat my food.

Robert Gillett

They don't care what they eat,
They'll take whatever they can hold,
Once in Newquay a cheeky fucker stole the wifes tuna roll.
(True story)

You hear the stories about the crazy one that nicked dave's pasty,
These fuckers are possessed and for food they get nasty.

These won't just shit on your car when you're driving through the slow lanes,
They'll line up on a lamp-post,
Wait for you and take aim.

So when you come to Cornwall,
Enjoy the delights,
I promise there's more than enough.
Just be mindful of the seagulls,
The buff ones with tattoos,
Chewing cigarette butts.

Having a poo

It's amazing what you do when you're having a poo.
It use to be a boring but sacred place,
Now you do so much more with that constipated face.
You sit on the bog with your phone in your grip,
You've got the whole outside world with you when you're taking a shit.
It's become the new norm,
Sitting and squeezing whilst filling out forms.
You can pay the council tax or your water bills,
Watch dumb videos for 3 second thrills.

You might Google,
Read random shit while you're having a shit get off the loo and you've forgotten all of it.
You'll catch up on that text you've been meaning to do,
Not telling them the only time you can make for them is when you're having a poo.

You're scrolling through social media just to see what's happening outside the toilet,
You're searching Twitter on the shitter,
Rolling down your Facebook feeds whilst you're giving it that extra squeeze,

You Tik tok while you plop.
You've got loo roll in one hand in the other checking Instagram,
You've become master multi tasker,
Swiping and wiping.

You put your phone on the side,
Still watching it while you wipe,
Washing your hands after getting off the throne,
You've now got water all over your phone,
Pulling up your pants you give it one last glance.
You look back at the toilet,
This time you're lucky you didn't drop it,
You take your phone and put it safely back in your pocket.

It used to be poop,
Wipe,
Wash,
Then out the door.

Your pooping ritual isn't so sacred anymore.

If looks could kill

If looks could kill,
5 times a day I'd probably be dead.
It could be something I might have done,
Maybe something that I said.

In the morning everyone is shattered but I tell my son to hurry up n get ready for school,
He turns into a demon and uses his eyes as a tool,
I didn't ask for a lot but his side eye death stare could have killed me on the spot.

I go and see my daughter,
The place is a mess,
So I tell her to tidy her room n boom,
I only told her to clean up the place
And she looks at me with the worst screw face,
She turns batshit crazy with those killer eyes,
I got out of this one unscathed,
I'm lucky to be alive.

At the shops I park in the disabled bay,
Pull out the blue badge and so I can be on my way,

Across the carpark I have these harrowing deathly eyes from this judgemental witch,
She soon looks at the floor when I step out with my stick.

At a zebra crossing I slowly walk across the road forcing this man has to abruptly stop,
It's not my fault but his eyes could have killed me on the spot.

At night,
At home,
I get unchanged,
Drop the blue ones,
Give the wife the eyes and ask if she's coming to bed,

If looks could kill,

I'd most certainly be dead.

Remember, remember

Remember, remember the 5th of November.
Does it work for everything? Remember your wife's birthday, the 10th of September.
So it would be Remember, remember the 5th of November and the 10th of September.

Your son's birthday and your daughter's birthday too? The 7th of December and the 25th of December.
Remember, remember the 5th of November, the 10th of September, the 7th and the 25th of December.
Is this an easy way to remember it?

Does it work for brothers and sisters too? 16th August, 13th July, 8th of May, 1st of September and the 14th of December.
It's getting busy but, remember, remember the 5th of November, The 10th of September, the 7th and the 25th of December, the 16th of August, 13th of July, 8th of May, the 1st of September and the 14th of December.

Nephew's birthdays and Nieces birthdays, 9th January,14th January, 18th and 31st May, 26th June and 21st of September.

Robert Gillett

Remember, remember the 5th of November, the 10th of September, the 7th and the 25th of December, the 16th of August, 13th of July, 8th of May, the 1st of September, the 14th of December, the 9th and the 14th January, 18th and 31st of May, the 26th of June and the 21st of September.

Parents and In-laws, 1st December, 1st June, 20 th and 24th September. That's everyone so, remember, remember the 5th of November, the 10th of September, the 7th and the 25th of December, the 16th of August, 13th of July, 8th of May, the 1st of September, the 14th of December, the 9th and the 14th January, 18th and 31st of May, the 26th of June, the 21st of September, 1st December, 1st June and the 20th and 24th September.

I got all the dates, I made the rhyme. It seems like a lot of work to remember. Maybe I should just remember remember the 5th of November and remember remember to look at the fucking calendar.

I don't like poetry

The teenage daughter's boyfriend

Your daughter gets a boyfriend,
She's growing up,
She's become a teen.
The last thing you wanna do is be mean.
Getting on her case,
Pushing her away,
Trying to educate her because you know what's best because you've been that teenage boyfriend,

You had that immature brain,
You ran around with your own little tallywacker,
You were stupid.
So he must be stupid because all teenage boys are stupid.
How are you supposed to deal with this because you can't trust teenage boys you know they all take the piss.

Do you ignore him?
Stare at him with killer eyes feeding the fear he has building inside.
Do you put him in a headlock, give him a monkey scrub and tell him this is only the start.
Let his imagination fester about the carnage you might cause if he breaks your daughter's heart.

Robert Gillett

Do you take him on a drive and explain you don't wanna be mean but if he breaks your daughter's heart you'll tie rocks around his feet and push him in the sea?
She's allowed to get away with murder but if he hurts her you might run him over.

Do you let him in your house?
That way you know she's safe,
Your alarms are on high alert so you're there just in case.
Do you keep that door open 3 inches wide,
Constantly popping your head inside.

You don't wanna make her a prisoner but you wish she'd go and live with Repunsal.
You wanna lock her away but she's gotta grow up one day and she's gonna wanna find love.
What do you do?
Maybe father up,
 Just shake her boyfriend's hand and give your daughter your trust.

I don't like poetry

Don't laugh

How am I supposed to be responsible and tell someone they're not funny when he always makes me laugh?
He's a clown and always entertaining us,
His mates,
His class.
It's my job to tell him it's not funny,
But how can I not laugh when he says to me "Dad, you're so ugly scooby doo couldn't solve that mystery"
Or "Dad, you're so dumb, you'd go to the dentist to turn on your Bluetooth"
Or "Dad, you're so dumb you'd go to the superbowl and take a spoon"
How can I tell him he's not funny?
He's in trouble at school because he doesn't understand that it's mean to call his bald teacher "Mr Clean".
Previously he got in trouble when Mr Clean told him to draw Professor Dumbledoor and he got out his pencil and drew a dumb door.
How is that not funny?
How can I not laugh?
The innocence of him is brilliant,
Oneday after school he got in the back of the car,
As cool as a cucumber he asked me,

Robert Gillett

"Dad, what comes after 69?"
I say 70,
He stares at me in the eyes and calmly replies
"no dad, after 69 comes mouthwash"

How can I tell him he's not funny?
That's so fucking hard,
My 10 year old son is always making me laugh.

That doesn't go there

The milk doesn't go in the microwave,
Butter doesn't go in the oven,
The nuts don't go in the fridge,
And the peas don't belong in the sink.

The cheese shouldn't be in the freezer,
Beans don't go in the toaster,
The coffee doesn't go with the tins,
And tomatoes don't go in the bin,

The juice doesn't get poured in the kettle,
Your wallet doesn't need washing up,
The phone don't go in the fruit bowl,
Your bag doesn't go in the cubby hole.

Your shades don't live in the loo,
The keys don't belong in the shoe.
I pretty sure there's a right place for these things,
But this brain fog has me losing everything.

Robert Gillett

Today is today

Today is today not yesterday last week,
These days get a little confusing for me.
The calendar says what's on,
But the right day is usually wrong.
The time says you're early but you missed the right day,
It's someone's party but I never know who's on what date.
I finally arrived somewhere but why am I here?
I follow my own instructions but my instructions ain't clear.
I get lost in me own house and put the shoes on the wrong feet,
Even though it seems like it,
I swear there's nothing wrong with me.

Today is today not yesterday last week,
I forget everything maybe it's lack of sleep,
It's the right time but I'm at the wrong place,
I've mistaken someone else because I've forgotten their face,
I shouldn't be here now but in two hours time,
Not sure I can keep blaming this stupid watch of mine.
I definitely should be somewhere but whom am I supposed to speak?
I dunno,
I forgot today is today, not yesterday last week.

Writing for support

Writing for support has been a big thing for me. I know it is for other people too. I've found, for me, this is one of the most important. There's been so many times I've needed support and someone else's words have helped me, not necessarily with poetry but still words from someone else.

You can send words of solidarity into the matrix we call life, maybe send out that message for others so they don't feel alone. Showing people that "Those things" are a normality for other people. Writing to raise awareness of something in particular or support someone's message can be so important and equally fulfilling.

If you've been following the book and my "Beneath The Tracksuit" journey as a whole, these are literally the reasons I began sharing my writing. My world would look very different if I didn't take a leap of faith and share my work, well I was pushed...

If you are able to captivate people with a verse you have written and use that to send a message, then only good can come from that.

You're still valid

Someone will always be happier than you,
Your happiness is still happiness too.
Someone will always be more depressed than you,
Your depression is still valid too.

Someone will always be more carefree than you,
You can still be carefree too.
Someone will always be more anxious than you,
Your anxiety is still valid too.

Someone will always be stronger than you,
You can still have strength too.
Someone will always be sicker than you,
Your illness is still valid too.

Someone may have life different to you,
You are allowed to have a life too.
Someone may struggle more in life,
It doesn't mean your struggles are not valid too.

Men know depression

Men don't show depression,
Afraid of the stigma that you are weak if your emotions should leak,
You're a soft bloke if you actually admit to someone you're feeling broke,
Men hide,
Keeping the pain inside,
Locking in the damage,
Burying it in the deepest parts of the mind.
Men know the fears of being seen as a clown and being shut down if you let your struggles out.
So men choose not to shout.
Men know depression.

It's unusual when you hear a man has been struggling for years but men feel the way it feels when you're holding back the tears.
Men know what it's like to cry,
The feeling inside leaving sadness weeping in the eyes,
The inner sighs,
The wanting to die.
Men understand the feeling of why,
Why!!!

Robert Gillett

Why am I broken?
Why has the world turned its back on me?
Why do I feel so empty?
Men know depression.

Men know the giving up.
Men know of the having enough,
They know the looking above with no religion
but still asking God why does this have to be so tough?
Men know the hurt,
They understand the heartbreak,
The struggles that leave the lingering ache.
Men know the broken waves of emotion,
Life with the mental corrosion,
Men are forever living forcing internal thought suppression,
You may not see it but men know depression.

There's no need for that

There's no need for that funny look,
You can't see what my disability has took.

There's no need for you to accuse,
You don't know the parts of my body that I struggle to use.

There's no need for you to whisper behind my back,
You're gossiping about me without understanding the facts.

There's no need for you to be rude,
You have no idea what my body goes through.

There's no need for your judgement of me,
My life is difficult enough without your thoughtless mentally.

Robert Gillett

Mental health

Mental health issues may seem irrelevant or have you joking but the feel of it's realism leaves people emotionally choking,

Low mood is trivial to you but it's an understatement of the destruction that someone is battling through,

Depression may be invisible to you but it's altered the reality of what someone's eyes choose to see,

Anxiety means nothing to you but it's got hearts racing, it's got panic inside that's internally draining, it's sending untrue thoughts driving someone crazy,

Suicidal thoughts may be unknown to you, that feeling of last hopes and final effort, the eventual giving in, lost in the broken aloneness is unknown to you but for someone it's true.

Mental health may seem insignificant to you but for someone else.....

My strength must survive

My struggle may seem managed,
Some might say my strength makes stresses minimal,
Simple.
My smile may seem magnificent,
Smiles mask so many signs.
My smile magically stores my struggle.
My sickness making scars,
My scrambled motor skills,
My shipwrecked mental state,
Masked.
So many struggles may shatter me,
Still my strength must survive,

Many stereotypicals make struggling mental states more severe.
My supporters make struggling minor,
Some make smiles memorable.
Support may secure my stability,
May save me.
Staying mentally strong must suffice.
My sanity may spiral,
Mental state may suffer,

Robert Gillett

My serenity may struggle,
My strength must survive.

Mistaken speech misaligns self motivation,
Shabby movements stupidly make standing more strenuous.
Menacing spasms make significantly more stresses,
My sleep misses so many stages.
Many symptoms may seem mighty strange,
Multiple Sclerosis might seem magnificently stranger,
Multiple Sclerosis makes simple measures severely monstrous,
Still my strength must survive.

A conversation

You don't need a knife.
There's nothing that can be that severe you need to be running around trying to take someone's life.
A blade in your hand doesn't make you a man,
You are more of a fool thinking that a 6 inch kitchen blade makes you look cool.
It doesn't.
You've taken too many steps down the wrong path,
You carry a blade because you think it's smart?
Because your friends do?
Because you're told it's a brave thing to do?
You're misguided bruv.
Don't let misconceptions get in your head.
Carrying that thing around is gonna end up with next man dead.
Someone's son or daughter, brother or sister,
Someone to be missed.
No one holds victory with this,
There's no trophies for putting bodies in the ground,
Only coffins will be lifted and lives will be shifted into depths of depression and loss,
A whole world becomes at loss,
One lifeless body is not the only cost.

Robert Gillett

Worlds become shattered.
An echo of broken emotions will travel through generations, along with the words about that beautiful soul snatched away because you went cold.
You will take your own life and leave it behind bars, filled with regrets.
A life of self disrespect and lost hope, praying for the forgiveness from which you don't deserve.
It's not a moment of madness or a mistake when you take the life of another with your own hands.
You took the power and it will be your plan.
Don't be that man, That's not who you are.
You're angry and broken and your hurt goes unspoken but I hear you!
Bruv I'm listening, The world should be listening!
Don't become a victim of the blade from poor decisions that you made in a moment of madness or be a consequence of the fear that can be solved with support,
Seriously bruv before you walk out the door remember a life is worth so much more,
Don't put that blade in your pocket,

Think about it.

Leave it in the drawer.

I don't like poetry

Fall in line

Living a life dissimilar to the typical,
Fighting against the grain,
My life is as important as any,
It's not my fault we're not the same.

I see things different to you,
My thought pattern is not "Atypical"
It's not that I'm wrong,
My feelings and thoughts are unpredictable.

I am always trying though,
It's difficult to live in the world you see,
It's feels strange to be something else,
I really just want to be me.

I promise I'm trying my best,
It's hard pretending all the time.
I don't understand what you expect,
It's not as simple as "Fall in line".

Some words for my son, neuro spicy living in a neurotypical world.

Robert Gillett

Writing for others

Writing poetry for others can be such an amazing thing to do. I'm not the best talker so I love how I can let my poetry flow and do the talking for me. I'm definitely so much better at taking my time and writing verses about someone than I am with instant vocals.

Whether you're writing about someone you know or writing a direct poem for someone, like a love poem, a little rhyme, a thank you or writing in memory of someone. I found it to be a nice release and a cool way to send emotions.

A poem for the wife is always a good shout. Putting things in a lovely way to express your feelings for someone will always be received in a positive way.

It's funny how you get a lot of "I don't like poetry" but at the same time people actively seek out lovely poems and sweet verses for their partners, parents, children ect in cards and things like that for celebrations.

You can write words for someone after they've died. I've done this a few times. I thought I could say to them words that I never got to say before they passed. It's brilliant for helping keep their memory alive and it's a nice thing to look back on for reminiscing.

You can write just about anything for just about anyone.

It can be an awesome gift to give to someone you care for or a great way to keep hold of a memory or you could be like the storytellers from hundreds of years ago and use poetry to record moments of historical importance.

I love you

I've watched you grow from a tiny heartbeat and your pattering feet,
Into the amazing people that now stand before me.
You've taken the challenges of life and you refuse to lose,
You won't be beaten or knocked down or be destroyed by the blues.
You stand tall, together in the mess, even though friends you are not the best, When it counts you're there.
You're there for me, your mother and each other, no separation in despair.
Proud parents of our growing children that are living the challenge of a neuro spicy life, taking it in your stride, living your lives with hearts of gold inside.
You are nothing short of inspirational.
Parenting is far from complete but for me, you have it all.
You are incredible and I will say it out loud because I am, as a father, insanely proud.
Thank you,
Both of you.
I love you.

My amazing children Phoenix and Miley.

Goodbye letter

Alright mate,
Are you listening?
I should have wrote to you sooner,
I don't need paper or stamps this time,
I've got no address for you,
I've not been too busy to write to you but I didn't what to say,
I need to let you know that you'll never be forgotten,
I carry you with me everywhere,
There's certain things I do and I can still see your face there.
It's like you've been following me,
You've been gone for years but I still feel you around.
You left too early but I know it wasn't your fault.
I went right and you went back,
You turned around on the packed that we made but I'm not mad at you for that,
I understand how it is.
I know how it is.
It's just a shame it got you and I wasn't there at the end,
I wish you'd have reached out,
You left too much behind,
You didn't only leave your friends behind,
You left your wife,

Robert Gillett

You left your son,
He has no choice but to grow without you,
She'll let him know who you really were not what you became because she knew you like I knew you,
I'm sorry we drifted but I didn't have a choice,
I didn't make them moves anymore,
I climbed out of that hole,
I left that world behind and with that world I left you.
I'm sorry I wasn't there and I'm sorry I didn't get to say goodbye,
I hope forgiveness for that isn't too late,
I hope when I get there you'll be waiting outside the gate.
For now goodbye my friend.

In loving memory Lee Youster.

I paint

Numb,
That feeling your insides go when diagnosed with an illness were the future looks frightening,
It looks cold.
Fingers are numb from that illness sucking the life from inside of you and you have no control.

Why?
How can I explain my pain when I don't know how to talk?
The verbal capability for that doesn't sit in the forefront of my damaged brain.

When I find the correct words no one listens or no-one can decipher the jumbled explanation of long medical statements that can actually describe what's happening to me.

So I paint,
I talk with my fingers and you listen with your eyes,
I paint to express the emotions that words cannot explain,
I paint to free my brain from the heartache and fear that grabs as it wishes,

Robert Gillett

My story is told on a canvas through an intense stream of colour,
Through my brushes my pain screams across the page,
You can't feel my pain without me needing to talk but I remain silent,
Yet my voice is louder than ever.

The world can know my story without speaking a single word,
Through my art I'm heard,
Through seeing my pain I will be heard.
Through your eyes you can hear me,
You can hear the damage,
The distress,
The depressing pressure I fight to survive,
My hands are numb but they glide and work like dark angel bringing my pain to life,
I'm numb,
My hands are numb,
My emotions run numb,
But I feel alive.

For my legendary mate Atom St George.

You saved me

You were there when I had nothing,
You were there when I had no money,
No prospects,
No illness,
Just a broken man with a dim future.
You helped build me after I crashed,
You lifted my confidence after it smashed.
You helped me rise out of the depressive hell hole I lived in before there was you,
You saved me from myself,
You saved me from my life,
You gave me a meaning and helped me put all that shit behind,
That was before the sickness,
You stuck by me when the disease took control,
Depression came again and started chipping at my soul,
But you stuck by me.
You watched me smoke and put it all away,
You watched me topple giving in to the drink,
You knew I was chasing white lines but you were still there begging me to think.
You saved me.

Robert Gillett

I fell off and it broke you,
I fell off and you taped me up before you.
You've always saved me from myself,
Right from the start,
We gelled together and you soon after stole my heart,
You watched my rise,
You watched me fall,
You watch me then gain a presence,
You help me build it all.
I went from a depressed lad,
To a broken man,
To helping people around the world,
I became an inspiration.
But it's you that deserves the admiration.
Without you there would be no BTT,
There'd be no Robbie,
I wouldn't be here if you weren't standing beside me.
I still live in a whirlwind of damage and you're there holding my hand,
The illness I have deletes me but you don't see a change in this man.
You saved me.

To my beautiful wifey Donna-Marie Gillett.

A better outlook

I said at the beginning "poetry was a game changer" I hope you can now see what I mean. The impact it's had on my life has definitely been positive. I'm more open than I was before, it may be in verse form but it works for me. It set me on a positive path for a career that I would have never have thought of because "I didn't like poetry" so why on earth why I have divulged into it as deep as I have.

It's been 4 years since I started writing poetry, putting words into verse. What a journey it's been so far. After becoming open with my emotions, using words opened a whole world for me. I've connected with people all over the world, I've been featured in multiple magazines, I have a spoken word album that's streamed daily all over the world. I performed at a major festival in the summer and I now run my own spoken word and poetry events to help get others reading, talking and expressing themselves on stage.

That's a million miles away from "I don't like poetry".

I'm not saying poetry is going to do that for everyone, far from it but I'd definitely recommend it as a tool, an outlet or even somewhere to go and have a laugh.

Robert Gillett

There's so much more to it than the boring, negative perspective that poetry holds in mainstream society. If we are honest it really doesn't deserve it.

Poetry is an art, just like painting, acting or music. These things don't have a general negative impact on society so why does poetry?

It doesn't make sense.

I can't say this book is going to change the world or the view of the masses but if it makes one person have a different opinion then that's a job well done and even if not, I'm glad you were here to read my story and hopefully you enjoyed the works throughout this book.

You don't like poetry

Saying you don't like poetry is the same as saying you don't like music or you don't like TV,
You shouldn't say you don't like poetry without listening to it,
Poetry isn't long, boring, uneventful rubbish that was written to please a king,
Poetry is anything,
Poetry It's in everything,
Of course you won't like all poetry but you don't like all music,
You don't like all TV,
You might love and dance to heavy metal rock music with a deep and dirty beat but hate intense classical music that does absolutely nothing for your feet,
You might love the ballets,
Those songs that has you hairs standing on end but detest the rap music because you don't understand it,
You think it makes no fucking sense,
But You still like music,
You just don't like all music,
You like TV, Movies, Superhero movies,
You might love Batman but think Iron man is an absolute bellend

Robert Gillett

You might love eastenders but hate the east enders on love Island,
Hate reality TV but love those David Atombougher wildlife documentaries but you don't hate TV.

Poetry is an art not a genre, poetry has its own genres,
Its own different kind of mind,

Love, Laughter, Emotional, Serious, Pointless, Stupid,
Engaging, The release of a soul, It's stories needed to be told,
A means to an end, A goodbye letter to that dead friend,

It's a new way to express and let go of some mental stress.
Explain away some pain or you can just play games
with words messing around in a pointless verse about nothing.

You can't dislike something you've never read,
You can't really have an opinion of something you don't even know,
Imagine going from "I don't like poetry"

4 years later.....

You put on a whole show!

For the record

You don't need a degree to read or write poetry. You don't have to fit a stereotypical box to enjoy it. Poetry is not for snobs and it ain't stupid. Poetry isn't boring, well some is but you quickly find out what type you don't like, just like music or TV.

There's loads of rules and styles and names for all different types of poetry. I respect the rules of poetry and there are some absolutely brilliant ways to write.

Hikau
Limerick
Couplets
Triplets
Free verse
Sonnets
This goes on and on and on and on but I'm far from a poetry teacher and I'm not even going to pretend I am. I just write.

I use the rules more as guidelines. It makes it more accessible, more fun. Let's be real, a few rules are meant to be broken.

Robert Gillett

I'm not a poetic genius, I'm not even educated in poetry, I'll never be the bard (special poet) of anywhere. I didn't study literature.

I just found a respect for an art and simply put words in a verse.

I now use it as the best tool to combat my mental health. I use it to make people think, to make light of complicated conversations and I use it to make people laugh.

I use poetry to connect, to speak out, to socialise, poetry actually became quite a thing for me.

I'm on my third book. I've got two pamphlets and I've made a spoken word album and my poetry is read, heard and spoken across the planet everyday.

The funny thing is though,

I don't like poetry.....

Special thanks

There's a whole list of people, and more that have been with me throughout this journey from a hidden, embarrassed, bedroom poet to an international selling, performance poet.

A special thank you to all here.

Mark Taylor-Moseley Thank you so much for the heads on how to write a book. I've managed to write 3 books, 2 pamphlets and a whole stage show with the technology that's in the palm of my hands and I would have never had a clue where to start without your help.

My good friend Jon Langford, for giving me the opportunity to share my poetry and work with you and others at skillshare and setting the wheels in motion which led me to began my work performing.

Dicky Souray - Sprout Spoken, for opening your stage to me and giving me major insight and advice on how to navigate as a performer. Thank you so much.

Tara, my fellow poet and inspiration, being there supporting me and backing me up along the way and introducing me to the stage, I'm so grateful for encouragement and support.

To the wonderful Mimi, from my first ever compère to the friend you became, thank you. You've supported me from my first performance and helped navigate the stage all the way to the host I am now. You even got me featured in two magazines, one of them I was on the cover. Thank you for everything.

Jen, Ruinarte. Working with you to be able to put some of my words into radio worthy music has been a delight. You managed to take my ever changing mind and still create an album with me, which is incredible. Our work together is played around the world daily and that is nothing short of amazing.

Adam, Atom St. George. My MS Warrior brother, Connecting with you through the arts we've both come to use as an outlet is definitely a highlight for me and has been nothing short of inspiring. They way you test my abilities and constantly push me to think outside of the box is always improving the way I work. I can't wait for our book!

My Beneath The Tracksuit family, your unwavering support with my illness has been incredible. Reading my words and letting me know that I am not alone in the struggle that this disability is. Being a listening ear when I'm fighting those hard days. You are all amazing. Thank you all so much.

My amazing kids, both of you have been so amazing and supportive through this journey. You've taken MS in your stride and you are both always there to help, support me and you're not even embarrassed your Dad's a poet! That's a big thing. Thank you both for being amazing.
I love you both so much.

Of course my beautiful wifey, Donna-Marie. Your support throughout this whole journey, from the first poem, the whole process, the ups and downs of mental health and the disability I fight, the disability we fight, has been second to none. You have shown me light in my dark days and have helped pull me up everytime. You're always there encouraging me and supporting me to be on stage and grow as an artist. I wouldn't have done this without you, I couldn't have done this without you. Thank you for everything. I love you more than any poem could say.

The poetry and contents written in this book were written by myself and are covered by the UK copyright laws.

All rights are reserved

Robert Gillett
Beneath the Tracksuit
2024 ©

Printed in Great Britain
by Amazon